The
HOLY GHOST
AND ME

ALSO BY JOY SEMIEN

Praying for Oranges: How to Believe for the Impossible

The
HOLY GHOST AND ME

30 DAY DEVOTION WITH THE CREATOR, THE SON, AND THE HOLY SPIRIT

JOY SEMIEN

Copyright © 2020 by Joy Semien

All rights reserved. No part of this book may be reproduced, distributed, or transmitted in any form or by any means, including photocopying, recording, or other electronic or mechanical methods, without the prior written permission of the author, except in the case of brief quotations embodied in reviews and certain other non-commercial uses permitted by copyright law.

Bible Gateway passage: New International Version. (n.d.). Retrieved November 28, 2020, from https://www.Biblegateway.com

Semien, J. (Director). (n.d.). *The Holy Ghost and Me Podcast* [Audio Video file]. Retrieved November 28, 2020, from https://open.spotify.com/show/6Eg77GUXbstAeOr1ete478

Publisher:
The Holy Ghost and Me
P.O. Box 562. Geismar, Louisiana 70734

Preface

Who is this book for?

This 4-week daily devotional seeks to guide the reader into strengthening their relationship with God, Jesus, and the Holy Ghost. The devotional is divided into four topic areas: (1) Learning to Follow the Holy Ghost, (2) Becoming a Certified Holy Ghost Warrior, (3) Stepping into Spiritual Maturity, and (4) Expecting Manifestations.

How to use this book?

This book is an easy read designed to help the reader develop their relationship with the Father while also providing daily reality checks. The book guides the reader through a 4-week journey consisting of daily scripture, devotion, question, challenge, and a prayer. This devotional is designed to be used during daily meditation as a supplemental biblical study to increase spiritual growth.

I Dedicate This Book To:

- My grandmother Leona who taught me to submit all my cares to the Lord and let Him fight my battles.
- My great-aunt Ophelia who taught me how to hone my God-given gift of encouraging and speaking to others.
- My apostle Leroy Thompson who gave me the foundation, I needed to understand my authority and dominion in the spiritual realm.
- My spiritual counselor Dr. Guthrie who taught me how to make wisdom my sister and understanding my next of kin (Proverbs 7:4).
- My writing coach Kristie F. Gauthreaux who encouraged me to write and publish my first Christian Devotional!
- My *Crazy Faith Holy Ghost Crew* who encourages me to follow my dreams and pushes me to work on my assignments from God.

Table of Contents

Prayer

A LETTER FROM THE AUTHOR 9

LEARNING TO FOLLOW THE HOLY GHOST 11

    Who is the Holy Ghost?
    Discerning the Voice of the Father
    Questions for the Holy Ghost
    Resting in the Holy Ghost
    Allowing the Holy Ghost to Break You
    Holy Ghost Revealed Gifts and Talents
    Holy Ghost Authority

BECOMING A CERTIFIED HOLY GHOST WARRIOR 29

    Warrior Get Up ... It's Time for Battle
    Establish Your Holy Ghost Crew
    Prayers of a Warrior
    Establish Your War Room & Battle Plan
    Stop Being a Lazy Warrior
    Scars of a Warrior

STEPPING INTO SPIRITUAL MATURITY... 47

    Honey It Is Time to Clean House
    Stop Playing Hercules
    Keys of Disappointments
    Blind Spots
    Drop the Anchor of Unforgiveness

  EXPECTING MANIFESTATIONS... 65
    The Wait
    Keep Your Hands Raised and Eyes on Him
    Stop Telling God What You're Ready For
    Mind God's Business
    Divine Confirmations
    Do Not Be So Easily Offended
    Full Circle Moments

SINNER'S PRAYER 83

A Letter from The Author

Dear Reader,

One of my favorite scriptures in the Bible is Psalm 27:10-11, which reads:

> *"Though my Father and mother forsake me, the Lord will receive me. Teach me your way, Lord; lead me in a straight path because of my oppressors."*

This scripture is filled with many hidden jewels.

- *Jewel #1:* Regardless of who leaves you, God will still be with you.
- *Jewel #2:* God will not turn his back on you.
- *Jewel #3:* God will teach you.
- *Jewel #4:* God will keep you from all those who seek to do you wrong.

These hidden jewels lay the underpinning of his love. Meaning that no matter what you do, God will always accept, cover, protect, and teach you - as his child. The third jewel lays the foundation for this book. Jewel number three says, "He will teach you." That is an immensely powerful statement. Regardless of the situation God will never leave you nor turn his back on you. God will never forsake you, but what HE WILL do is TEACH YOU through His spirit!

After Jesus's death, resurrection, and ascension Christ sent a helper called the Holy Spirit to live on the inside of you. The Holy Spirit, God's spirit, is here to help you with life challenges. The moment you accepted Jesus as your Lord and Savior; you permitted the Holy Spirit to live within you - to guide you to reach levels of spiritual maturity. In one way, it is almost like you are on an adventure with the Holy Spirit. Just you and the Holy Ghost hence "The Holy Ghost and Me."

Throughout this book, you will find tools and challenges that enables you to follow the Holy Ghost. I pray that this book blesses you and encourages you to follow the Holy Ghost!

Enjoy!

Week 1

Learning to Follow the Holy Ghost

Who is The Holy Ghost?

"And I will ask the Father, and he will give you another Advocate, who will never leave you. He is the Holy Spirit, who leads into all truth. The world cannot receive him because it is not looking for him and does not recognize him. But you know him because he lives with you now and later will be in you." – John 14:16-17

The Holy Spirit or the Holy Ghost is the very essence of God's spirit sent here post-Christ ascension. He is described as a helper and an advocate in John 14:16-17 also referred to as God's presence. The Holy Spirit is loyal, powerful, and sustaining.

Philippians 2:13 says God's energy lives in us. This energy is the Holy Spirit, where God's presence lives. He is a spirit tasked with walking with you, comforting you, and interceding to the Father on your behalf. Through Him comes keys of wisdom and understanding to unlock every locked door in your life.

The Bible instructs God's children to consult Him daily. As a child of God, you must ask Him for wisdom in everything you do or seek to do. Consult the Holy Spirit just like you would do with your best friend. God wants you to consult with him and ask him for help. Today I challenge you to spend time **consulting** God's spirit and **waiting** for direction.

Today's Challenge

Today I challenge you to look for the presence of the Holy Ghost.

You will know his presence because it is filled with peace, joy, hope, favor, creative power, transformation, freedom, and wisdom.

Once you identify his presence begin to follow it all day long – seeking his face and allowing him to guide you through every challenge whether good, bad, or ugly.

How will you seek to find God's presence today?

_____

_____

_____

_____

How will you commit to following God's presence today?

_____

_____

_____

_____

A Prayer for Today

Dear Father,

I want more of your Holy Spirit to pour into me - guide me in ways only you can. Grant me a personal prayer language that only you can understand so that I may draw closer to you. Lord, help me to recognize your presence and help me to hear your voice louder than I have ever heard it before. God give me the boldness I need to follow Your voice. Lord, help me to move when you say move, give me a willingness to be obedient, and seek your face. Lord, I love you, and I thank you for all you do on my behalf. I thank you that I am growing into who you destined me to be and that you are teaching me to follow the way of the Holy Ghost. In Jesus's name, I pray, Amen!

Discerning the Voice of the Father

"For I know the plans I have for you," says the Lord. "They are plans for good and not for disaster, to give you a future and a hope. In those days when you pray, I will listen. If you look for me wholeheartedly, you will find me." – Jeremiah 29:11-13

Discerning the voice of the Father is simple, but it comes from a relationship. Many people associate relationship with God and religion as one and the same. However, relationship is getting to know God on an intimate level while religion is just practicing spirituality (i.e., going to church). It is important that you establish a relationship not just checkboxes needed to achieve religious practices.

The more you spend time with God and seek His face, the more you can clearly recognize His voice. Like in the natural, the more you spend time with your parents, the more you understand their tones.

Today's Challenge

Identify the ways that God speaks to you.

Get to a place in your life that you stop begging God to answer your prayers and start seeking his face because he is your Father.

You should desire to draw close to him. The more time you spend in his presence, the more his voice will become recognizable.

Those tones indicate whether you should run to them because you did something wrong or to walk light-heartedly with laughter because your parents are about to give you some good news. The same is true for God. The more time you spend with God, the more time you learn to hear his voice. If you have a hard time hearing God's voice, try inviting him into the conversation – listening for his response. God is always speaking, but you are not always listening or paying attention. So today I challenge you to **shut up**, **pray**, and **listen** for his response.

Practical Steps to Discern Gods Voice

1. God speaks verbally to your spirit. Listen for a whisper in your spirit. Some people call this whisper the conscience, but Christians call this whisper the Holy Spirit. This whisper will help to guide your every move.
2. God speaks through people. He uses people to confirm what he is saying to you verbally. This typically happens without you even asking for advice or telling a person your business.
3. God speaks through open visions and/or dreams. He will allow you to see a picture/image of something - just like he did for Daniel in the Bible.
4. God speaks nonverbal (i.e., with a sign on the Interstate or a little sparrow). You can also ask God for a sign, like Gideon (Judges 6-8), to confirm his whisper.

How does the Holy Spirit speak to you?

_____

_____

_____

_____

A Prayer for Today

Dear Adonai (Lord),

Give me ears to hear your voice, a heart to receive what you have for me, and the wisdom to move in the direction you have called me to be. In Jesus Name, I pray, Amen!

Questions for the Holy Ghost

"Ask me and I will tell you remarkable secrets you do not know about things to come."– Jeremiah 33:3

The bible says in Jeremiah 33:3 ask God for whatever concerns you, and he will show you what is ahead.

The bible says the moment you accept Jesus as your Savior and God as your Father you become his child! This means that you now have divine access to your Father's heart.

Just like a child in the natural possesses a sense of curiosity so do children of God. Children in the natural are curious - they often boldly ask a gazillion questions to almost anyone who will listen. If the child feels safe, you can be sure that a question will be asked soon enough.

Today's Challenge

1. Do not be afraid to get vulnerable and ask God questions... He will answer you.
2. Have a heart to receive the answer regardless of how difficult it may be to receive.
3. Do not go looking for the answer - allow God to reveal it to you in his timing.
4. DO NOT TAKE UNSOLICITED HOLY GHOST ADVICE! If God did not give it Reject, it!

As God's child, you should feel safe enough to come to his throne room and boldly ask him questions. Now just like any parent he may not answer you or the answer that he provides may not be what you are looking for but be sure that he hears your cry.

Your father is waiting for you to have an intimate conversation with him. I challenge you today to **go boldly** to the throne, **talk** to God, tell him what is on your heart, and **expect** him to show you the hidden answers.

What is on your heart today? Is there something that you need to ask God today? Start here and release what is on your heart.

_____

_____

_____

_____

Vulnerability starts with honesty. Get Honest with God today. How are you feeling?

_____

_____

_____

A Prayer for Today

Dear Father God,

Help me to seek your face. Give me an ear to hear your heart and a heart that continuously longs for you. Help me to become vulnerable with you. Wrap me in your peace so that I may ask you the questions within the depths of my heart. Lord, give me the heart to receive whatever the answer is that I so desire to know. Teach me to wait on you today even amid what I presume as uncertainty. You know all things so help me to trust you. I pray this in Jesus' name, Amen.

Resting in the Holy Ghost

"Don't be afraid!" Elisha told him. "For there are more on our side than on theirs!" Then Elisha prayed, "O Lord, open his eyes and let him see!" The Lord opened the young man's eyes, and when he looked up, he saw that the hillside around Elisha was filled with horses and chariots of fire."– 2 Kings 6:16–17

Daily, you need to find yourself in an uncompromising position of rest. Sitting in a position of rest creates peace. As you find this position of rest you will soon find that no problem, situation, or individual can destroy your daily peace.

> **Today's Challenge**
>
> Take an uncompromising position of rest. Sit on your spiritual front porch, in your Holy Ghost Rocker, with your Holy Ghost Licensed shotgun, drinking your iced tea, ready to blast any enemy that tries to mess with your peace!

Finding rest is especially important during the battle season. Rest is the key to any good fight because fighting tired creates blind spots. Taking-up an unbothered position of rest with your eyes focused on Christ gives you time to worship your Father while giving your angels space to fight the battle on your behalf. The more you draw near to God the easier it is to take-up an <u>uncompromising position of rest</u>.

Taking-up an uncompromising position of rest is like watching a wise person of age sit on their front porch with a shotgun waiting for somebody to trespass. We must be like that in the spirit: wake up and decide to walk out onto your spiritual front porch, sit in your Holy Ghost Rocking Chair, with a Holy Ghost Licensed Shotgun of Faith ready to blast any demon in Hell that tries to steal your peace! Oh, do not forget the ice-tea (the Word of God). The more you sip on that tea, the more you will find yourself refreshed and prepared to blow the enemy off your territory (with prayer, praise, and worship)! Today be at **rest**!

How do you plan to take a position of unbothered rest today?

_____

_____

_____

_____

_____

_____

_____

A Prayer for Today

Dear El Elyon (God Most High),

Teach me to sit in your presence, taking-up an unbothered position of rest. Lord, thank you that no weapon formed against me shall prosper and that I am more than a conqueror. I thank you that there is a hedge of protection around me, and nothing and no-one will come in my way. I stand against every stronghold and every demonic force that is trying to attack me. Lord, I yield to you, and I take-up an uncompromising position of rest. In Jesus' name, I pray, Amen.

Allow the Holy Ghost to Break You

"This left Jacob all alone in the camp, and a man came and wrestled with him until the dawn began to break. When the man saw that he would *not win the match, he touched Jacob's hip and wrenched it out of its socket.* Then the *man said, "Let me go, for the dawn is breaking!"* But Jacob said, *"I will not let you go unless you bless me..."*– Genesis 32: 24-26

In life, everyone goes through a season of breaking, often filled with lots of pain and hardship. Also known as the Job syndrome. Though hard to endure in the beginning the end typically leads to new levels of maturity, wisdom, and blessings.

This season of breaking is like a skilled chef breaking open an egg. Initially, when the chef cracks the egg over a fire it looks like a runny mess with no purpose, but as the chef adds key ingredients, it manifests into a whole new creation, an omelet.

Today's Challenge

Seek Gods face and ask him what areas in your life still needs to be broken. As he reveals it to you allow him to break you so he can mature you.

When you go through a season of breaking the master chef is just making you into his omelet of a masterpiece. The more you seek God's face in this season and the stronger your relationship with him grows. As the relationship grows then God can expose various levels of gifts, talents, and creativity within you that were hidden away like little jewels. Everything you need to be successful in life is already on the inside of you; it just needs a little breaking and a little heat exposure. Today, **expect** the master chef, God, to **cook you** into an omelet – **extracting** your hidden talents, gifts, and creativity.

Describe an area in your life that you refuse to allow God to break for his glory.

_____

_____

_____

_____

_____

_____

_____

_____

A Prayer for Today

Dear Yahweh- Nissi (Lord My Banner),

I surrender all that I am to you. I ask that whatever is in my life that needs to be removed that you break it out of me today. Lord I desire to grow fully in you, but I know that requires an internal breaking. Lord, I permit you to cook me into your masterpiece. Use me for Your glory so all can see just how wonderful you are as my Father! In Jesus' name, I pray, Amen.

Holy Ghost Revealed Gifts and Talents

"God gave these four young men an unusual aptitude for understanding every aspect of literature and wisdom. And God gave Daniel the special ability to interpret the meanings of visions and dreams". Daniel 1:17

The moment you were created in your mother's wombs, small packages were deposited on the inside of your spirit. Each package contained a gift or a talent that would eventually aid you in operating in your purpose. Every living person has gifts and talents on the inside of them.

Today's Challenge

Ask God to un-cover your gifts and talents as well as give you the tools needed to apply them in activating your purpose.

The moment you accept Jesus into your life and welcome the Holy Ghost to live on the inside of you, he begins to pull out those gifts and talents, perfecting you according to his will. The closer you grow in relation to God, the more he reveals those gifts and talents.

God will often begin to reveal your gifts and talents before he places you in a position to use your gifts and talents. As those gifts and talents are uncovered, God through the Holy Ghost will teach you how to use each gift and talent. Once God feels that you have reached maturity then He will place you in the right position so that you can flourish. Today ask God to **reveal** your gifts and talents so that you can use each one of them for his Glory.

Write down at least three gifts and three talents you know that you possess. After you write them down then think about how you can use them to make a difference in your world.

Gifts	Talents	Difference Maker

A Prayer for Today

Dear Yahweh-Bore (Lord My Creator),

Reveal my gifts and talents to me so that I may use them in advancing your kingdom. Lord, help me to draw near to you. Cultivate every gift and talent that is on the inside of me – keep me grounded in you that I may stay humble and always give you honor. In Jesus' name, I pray, Amen.

Holy Ghost Authority

"Look, I have given you authority over all the power of the enemy, and you can walk among snakes and scorpions and crush them. Nothing will injure you." *Luke 10:19*

Every child of a king possesses a level of authority and dominion. That authority can produce, alter, and change destinies. They can also stand against enemies and take new territories.

As children of the most High God, you have a level of spiritual authority and dominion that you can utilize at any given time. This authority grants you the power to bring heaven's promises down to Earth (Matthew 16:19).

Today's Challenge

Locate any area in your life where you have become complacent.

Ask yourself if the complacency is linked to an awaited promise or an enemy attack.

Enter your prayer closet and stay there until you feel Gods presence overtake your complacency.

The key to operating in this authority is knowing who you are, whose you are, and what promises are yours to access. The Bible is full of promises and keys that can be used to stand against demonic principalities.

In other words, you do not have to accept the things you cannot change. You have the authority to stand on the promises of God, declare, and decree a thing knowing that the situation will work out for your good and God's Glory! Today I challenge you to activate your **kingdom authority** and **dominion** – make a declaration and expect it to manifest!

Identify areas in your life where you have grown complacent. Identify actions you can use to grow from complacency.

Complacency	Action

Identify four scriptures in the bible that grants you a specific authority. Identify the scripture and authority.

Scripture	Authority

A Prayer for Today

Dear Christos (Anointed One),

Show me how to activate the authority and dominion I possess to call things as though they should be! Teach me to follow you so that I may win every battle I face today! In Jesus' name, I pray, Amen.

Weekly Declarations

1. I Declare that this week I will follow the Holy Ghost!
2. I Declare that every day I am drawing closer to God!
3. I Declare that I allow God to draw out the hidden gifts and talents on the inside of me!
4. I Declare that I am humble!
5. I Declare that I live in an unbothered position of rest!
6. I Declare that I will become vulnerable before God and allow him to mature me into the person I was always designed to be!
7. I Declare that I can hear God's voice loud and clear!
8. I Declare that I follow God's voice!
9. I Declare that I wait patiently for Gods Direction!
10. I Declare that I am obedient and that I have the mind of Christ!

Write your own Declarations here...

1.

2.

3.

4.

5.

6.

7.

8.

9.

10.

Week 2

Becoming a Certified Holy Ghost Warrior

Warrior Get Up … It's Time for Battle!

"But in that coming day no weapon turned against you will succeed. You will silence every voice raised up to accuse you. These benefits are enjoyed by the servants of the Lord; their vindication will come from me. I, the Lord, have spoken!"- Isiah 54:17

People often run away from the promises they were called to possess often because of fear, anger, or just laziness. Get to the point where you stop allowing the devil to chase you out of your God-given territories.

Today's Challenge

Get up and fight! Whatever is coming against you be bold enough to look it in the eyes and declare victory!

As a warrior, you must decide if you are going to run or fight. If you decide to fight be ready to take authority of your territory ---DO NOT LET, the devil punk you out of what God has already given you! If God has confirmed in your spirit that something belongs to you, look the devil in his ugly little face and you tell him and his minions to GET THE HELL OUT OF YOUR WAY and GET THE HELL FROM YOU! He has no power! Get on your knees and fight for what is yours! When you know, something belongs to you – then claim it (Job 22:28).

Whatever you are believing for today call the battle won, give God all the glory, and the praise! You are built for this moment. Do not allow fear or uncertainty to move you from the place you know you are destined to be, even if the promise looks a little dusty. One more thing remember you are a child of the King so **DO NOT TAKE UNSOLICITED HOLY GHOST ADVICE**!! Get direction from God not man! Today I challenge you to **shake off** the dust, **rise-up** like a warrior and **fight** with your hands raised.

What is keeping you from becoming the warrior you are destined to be?

_____

_____

_____

_____

_____

A Prayer for Today

Dear El Shaddai (God Almighty),

Help me to stop allowing the devil to punk me out of my blessings. God, I know I am your child, which means I am a child of a mighty King. I know that I am equipped to be an undefeated warrior. Lord, help me to rise-up when the enemy attacks and attack back with your Word! Lord, reveal to me my identity so when it is time for battle, I can fight from a place of victory not fear! Lord continue to teach me to fight on my knees with my hands raised to thee! Father, I love you so much and I thank you for maturing me into who you designed me to be! In Jesus' name, I pray, Amen.

Establish Your War Room & Battle Plan

"But when you pray, go away by yourself, shut the door behind you, and pray to your Father in private. Then your Father, who sees everything, will reward you." - Matthew 6:6

Every mighty warrior needs a war room for strategizing a secret plan of attack. The room allows you to come up with a plan to kick and crush your enemy's head.

Today's Challenge

Set up your war room and ask God to help you build your battle plan!

As a Christian, you should seek to go into your inner room, get in prayer, and allow God to give you a battle plan. This room should be a room away from all distractions – a place where you can commune with God and seek his face.

Victorious warriors also know the key to win any battle is to have a battle plan! This plan must be full of scriptures that indicate who you are in Christ, the authority you possess, and the promises God has already given you. The more you commune with God by opening your Bible and praying, God will give you a battle plan you never knew existed. He will open doors no man can close and warn you about traps set-up by the enemy. Today, if you want to have an immediate advantage over the enemy in your battle **stop wasting time, start fasting, and start praying**. As a child of God, you have access to the Word of God - designed to develop your skills for battle – use them!

A Prayer for Today

Dear Elohim (Creator),

Give me fresh strategies to defeat the devil. Lord as storms roll into my life give me the wisdom to fight on my knees and seek your face. Lord help me to seek the word and develop a Battle Plan that I can use to defeat the devil. In Jesus' name, I pray, amen.

Find Scriptures you can add to your battle plan.

Scriptures	Memorized (Yes/No)	Added to Battle Plan (Yes/No)

Stop Being a Lazy Warrior

"Then he returned to the disciples and found them asleep. He said to Peter, "Couldn't you watch with me even one hour? Keep watch and pray, so that you will not give in to temptation. For the spirit is willing, but the body is weak!" – Matthew 26:40-41

The simplest definition of a Christian is being "like Christ" or "Christ-like." The expectation is to follow the ways of Christ and live a life of excellence. Part of living a life of excellence is to be diligent and not lazy!

Today's Challenge

Stop being a lazy warrior. You are hindering Gods movement.

The disciples in Matthew 26 found this out the hard way when they slept instead of praying like Jesus had asked. That one-hour of laziness was critical of the influence they had on Jesus' death and resurrection. At times you can be just like the disciples lazy, sleepy, and caught up on your own needs that you miss when God is trying to get your attention. God wants you to move in obedience even if it is an inconvenience. A divine inconvenience is an activation code needed to release a blessing. In other words, be obedient!

Remember laziness can keep you from the places God seeks to elevate you. Laziness fueled by the refusal or delay in obedience can lead to a hindrance to God's movement in the earth realm. Your delay or rejection in obedience to pray for someone, sow into someone, or move when God tells you to do something creates delays and traffic jams in the spirit. Refusing to move when your heavenly father asks you to can delay his manifestations in your own life and in others. Even if God asks you to do something and it inconveniences you to be sure to do it anyway! Do not be the cause of a spiritual traffic jam! Today I challenge you to **do whatever God asks you to do** even if you feel like it is an inconvenience.

Use this section to identify the areas in your life where you have been a lazy warrior and its origin.

Laziness	Origin	Plans to Build Diligence

A Prayer for Today

Dear El Shaddai (God Almighty),

I declare that the devil has no power over my life. I rebuke the spirit of lethargies, laziness, complacency, and pride off my life! Lord teach me to move the moment you called me to move. Teach me to use what I have so that I may honor you. Lord help me to be willing and obedient moving in boldness to complete what you have for me. Lord, I thank you for using me in this season. Lord help me to become a change agent for your kingdom! In Jesus' name, I pray, amen!

Healing the Wounds of a Warrior

"He heals the brokenhearted and bandages their wounds." - Psalm 147:3

Every warrior becomes wounded at some point on the battlefield. The healing of that wound is integral to prevent infection, amputation, and even death.

Your spiritual life is remarkably similar. In the spirit soul wounds can lead to lack of promotions, hindered blessings, stress, anxiety, fear, worry, and so much more. The more you run from something, or you try and cover it up, that very thing will come back to torment you — eventually moving you from the very place you were called to be. Do not allow your wound to become infected.

> **Today's Challenge**
>
> Ask God to show you your soul wounds. Get vulnerable with God and allow him to unpack your suitcase of pain, guilt, and discontentment.

As you obtain new or identify old soul-wounds in your life seek God first. Go into your prayer closet and ask him to begin the healing process so that the wound can properly heal. Immediately consult the Holy Ghost for healing. In some cases, it may be necessary to even tap into a spiritual counselor.

As you begin to heal seek forgiveness, repentance, asking God to completely heal the hurt in your heart. Stop walking away from your pain, pretending it does not hurt. Acknowledge your pain, get vulnerable with God, and present it to the Father so that he may begin to heal you fully. Remember a wound that is not properly cared-for causes infection and lasting damage. Only God can prevent infection. Today **get vulnerable** and **release all the pain** to the greatest Doctor and expect supernatural healing!

Use this section to identify the soul wounds you have in your life. Get Vulnerable and then ask God to heal every wound.

Soul-wound	Origin	Healing Scriptures

A Prayer for Today

Dear Abba Father,

At times I feel so broken. I have wounds deeper than I know how to reveal. Lord search me and help me to become who you destined me to be. I know that I cannot reach spiritual maturity until you have cleaned out my soul wounds. God help me to get vulnerable with you - then help me to let you heal me. Lord I release all my pain and hurt to you today! Heal me, God! I surrender! In Jesus' name, I pray, Amen!

Scars of a Warrior

"Nevertheless, the time will come when I will heal Jerusalem's wounds and give it prosperity and true peace." - Jeremiah 33:6

Old wounds healed improperly turn into scars. Scars then serve as a reminder of the original injury and the pain associated with the damaging incident. Although some scars can provide a testament to the challenges you have overcome, other scars remind you of the pain you had to endure.

Today's Challenge

Identify the scars in your life and allow God to show you how those scars are just a setup for a step-up!

Spiritual scars are like physical scars. Spiritual scars are reminders of unhealed soul-wounds. Evidence of improperly healed soul-wounds consists of depression, anxiety, worry, and physical illness. The only way to truly heal a spiritual scar is by applying spiritual healing cream, which contains vulnerability, forgiveness, serving others, and writing a vision for your future.

As healing begins to flow into your spirit, old scars will soon turn into testimonies with a badge of honor. Those testaments can then serve as the very thing God uses to bring people into his kingdom. Scars left untreated can block you from entering places of maturity and elevation. Be careful not to carry the hurts and pains associated with unwanted scarring with you - instead, allow those scars to serve as a reminder of the battles you have already won. Do not be afraid to show people your scars – use your scars as a testament to let others know they are also destined to win battles. Let them know that **the devil has no power** and that **they are overcomers**. Today allow the Holy Ghost to guide you in sharing your testimony!

Do you have old scars that need tending? Use this space to unpack your scars and turn them into testimonies.

Scars	Healing Scriptures	Testimony

A Prayer for Today

Dear Yahweh Rapha (Lord That Healeth),

Teach me how to use my scars to represent your kingdom. Allow my imperfections to be a testament of your glory to draw people into your kingdom. Identify individuals you would like for me to show my scars. God, give me the ability to speak about my scars with ease and help me to seek your healing power. Lord, I love you, and thank you for healing every scar that I have inside me. In Jesus' name, I pray, Amen.

Weekly Declarations

1. I Declare that I am becoming a certified Holy Ghost Warrior!

2. I Declare that I am Gods masterpiece and I have a pure heart!

3. I Declare that this week I will activate my God given authority!

4. I Declare that this week I will activate my God given dominion!

5. I Declare that I will win every battle set in front of me!

6. I Declare that I will stand against all the attacks of the enemy in prayer, praise, and worship! The battle is already won!

7. I Declare that no weapon formed against me shall prosper!

8. I Declare that every battle wound is healed!

9. I Declare that every scar has been turned into a testimony!

10. I Declare that I am diligent and not lazy!

Write your own Declarations here…

1.

2.

3.

4.

5.

6.

7.

8.

9.

10.

Week 3

Stepping into Spiritual Maturity

Honey it is Time to Clean House

"But if we confess our sins to him, he is faithful and just to forgive us our sins and to cleanse us from all wickedness." - 1 John 1:9

The beginning of spring is often a time for decluttering and disinfecting your home. During this season, you may throw out things to make space for items you no longer need.

Like spring cleaning in the natural, it is imperative that you declutter your spiritual house (heart and mind).

Today's Challenge

Allow God to clean every aspect of your house today (i.e., friends, family, soul wounds etc.). Allow God to come in and clean you out so you can begin to mature.

One indicator that you need to clean house is when your emotions are all over the place. If you find yourself emotionally unstable, then you know it is time to clean house. To clean your spiritual house, you must call your housekeeper Jesus and ask him to come clean your spiritual, mental, and physical houses so you can grow in him. In other words, invite God into your heart and mind - allow Him to clean out all the junk. Today take the time to **declutter your spiritual house**. Ask God to **transform** your heart and mind!

A Prayer for Today

Father God,

Help me to clean my spiritual house today. Remove all remaining soul wounds and people in my life who are preventing me from maturing. God give me the ability to immediately release everything that is not giving you glory. Help me to manifest my purpose with an accelerated speed now that I have released the dead weight. In Jesus' name, I pray, Amen.

Write down some areas in your life where you want God to help you clean you out spiritually (i.e., friends, emotions, responsibilities)?

_____

_____

_____

_____

Now, organize those things in terms of high priority or low priority by placing them in the house. High priority items should be placed upstairs while low priority items should be placed downstairs.

What are you Afraid of?

"For God has not given us a spirit of fear and timidity, but of power, love, and self-discipline." – 2 Timothy 1:7

Fear is FALSE, EVIDENCE, APPEARING, REAL! If not dealt with appropriately, fear can stop you from progressing to the places God has permitted you to access. Fear can scare you into disobedience – where you stop doing what God called you to do.

Today's Challenge

Do not let fear stop you! Conduct a fear inventory and then go out and do one thing on your fear inventory that gives God the glory!

The thing about fear is if you let it, this concept can paralyze you from achieving your purpose and reaching your destiny. Fear is just one way the devil tries to control you, and if you do not watch it, fear can control your entire life, and your thought processes, hindering you from reaching your destiny.

To truly walk-in maturity, you need to conduct an emotional inventory and unpack the areas in your life that increase your worries and anxieties. To conduct an emotional inventory, write down everything that makes you upset, happy, scared, anxious, or irritated. Then unpack their origins; this can help you get to the core of what has hindered you from reaching your full potential. An emotional inventory allows you to see that most of the things you fear are irrational and out of your control. Today I challenge you to **conduct an emotional inventory**.

A Prayer for Today

Dear Yahweh-Tsidkenu (Lord My Righteousness),

I submit all my emotions over to you – show me how to proceed in your will. In Jesus' name, I pray, Amen.

Conduct an Emotional Inventory.

I Am afraid to…	Why?

I Am happy/sad when …	Why?

I Am anxious/worried when…	Why?

Who Told You, that You were Naked?

"Who told you that you were naked?" the Lord God asked. "Have you eaten from the tree whose fruit I commanded you not to eat?" – Genesis 3:11

Nakedness is a feeling of shame, first felt in the Garden of Eden. This feeling came about after the devil whispered in Eve's ear that she was missing something.

Today's Challenge

Identify who was the first person in your life that told you that you were naked.

In one sense, the enemy pulled at Eve's insecurities and curiosities leading her away from the very places God had called her to occupy. The enemy told her lies, which led to her feeling naked and ashamed – running from the once intimate relationship she had with the creator.

Today I ask you who told you that you were naked? What are you ashamed of? What insecurities do you possess? What has the devil lied to you about preventing you from doing what God has called you to do? Was it a teacher, a family member, a friend, or a boss that told you that you were incapable? Did you believe them? Better yet, did you lie to yourself and say that you would never be successful?

When you are not secure in your calling, then you will allow the enemy to remove you from the very places God has called you. The more secured you become, the stronger you become, and the less likely you will be to fall to the hands of the enemy. So, tell the devil BYE FELICIA! Realize that your nakedness is God's love in its purest form. Stop letting other people shame you from the gifts that God has given you! Shake off the insecurities! Today take the time to **identify your insecurities** and ask God to heal you! **Do not let the devil punk you out of your blessings**! Realize God has the last say so and you will come out on top! The devil is full of lies! Now, go be great!

In what areas do you most feel naked? Who was the first person who told you, that you were naked? How can you use your nakedness to benefit the kingdom?

I feel naked when...	What/Who first made you feel this way?	Kingdom Purpose

A Prayer for Today

Dear El Roi (God Who Sees),

I ask that you give me wisdom and understanding to unpack every area of shame in my life. Reveal to me the places that I have covered and refuse to let you in. Reveal to me the mislabeled areas in my life where others called bad, but you called good. Lord block the hand of the enemy on my life, set me apart, and elevate me to the places I am destined to be. Lord, teach me to follow you in all that I do! In Jesus' name, I pray, Amen!

Stop Playing Hercules

"For he will order his angels to protect you wherever you go. They will hold you up with their hands, *so you won't even hurt your foot on a stone.*" – Psalm 91: 11-12

If you have ever watched the Disney movie or studied Greek mythology, you know of the Greek god Hercules, who was tasked with holding up the world on his own. If you are trying to do the same thing, this is called the *Hercules syndrome*.

Today's Challenge

Identify all the unnecessary weight that you are carrying in your life and drop it.

If not treated in its early stages, the *Hercules syndrome* will trick you into trying to carry the weight of YOUR world on YOUR shoulders. That weight will consist of an abundance of stress, financial problems, family sickness, sorrows, insecurities, and pains. The *Hercules syndrome* will fool you into trying to figure out who, what, when, where, and why. You will even try to solve all the problems by yourself – instead of giving it to God. The truth is, you are not Hercules, and you do not have super strength. So, give the weight to God!

As a child of the King, the angels oversee your protection. Their job is to ensure that you do not stumble and that you take steps to achieve your destiny! So why carry the unnecessary weight that will slow you down from reaching the places God has for you to overtake? As daughters and sons of the King, you are designed to walk weightless through the kingdom, using your authority to combat the devil and all his attacks! Your job is to surrender all your weight to God, so you do not have to carry it. Matthew 11:28 tells you that you can go to God if you are weary and exchange your heavy weight for his light weight! Today I challenge you to **release the weight** and follow Christ!

What weight do you need release over to God? Write that out here and then ask God to exchange his light weight for your heavy weight.

_____

_____

_____

_____

_____

_____

_____

A Prayer for Today

Dear Jehovah- Jireh (Lord My Provider),

I need your help! This weight that I am carrying is too heavy. I am growing weary. At times I am emotionally unstable due to all the stress, that I try to carry on my own. Lord, today I surrender all this weight to you. Lord, teach me to seek your face before I pick up unnecessary baggage. Teach me to shake off the things that are not of you so that I may excel in the things that you have designed me to be. Lord, teach me to follow you. In Jesus' name, I pray, Amen.

Keys of Disappointments

"For I know the plans I have for you," says the Lord. "They are plans for good and not for disaster, to give you a future and a hope." Jeremiah 29:11

Disappointments are inevitable; they can come from a parent, a friend, a family member, a teacher, a boss, God, or even an enemy. Disappointments can leave you feeling abandoned, lonely, and even forgotten.

Today's Challenge

Empty your key ring from keys of disappointments. Allow God to protect you and vindicate you. Stay in your prayer closet and allow God to give you keys of satisfaction.

As you experience disappointments, it is a strong possibility that you will begin to develop a self-built protective wall designed to keep you from experiencing the pain of getting hurt again. If not dealt with in its origin, the wall of disappointments will stop you from excelling! This wall will create selfishness and pride in your life, blocking your spiritual growth.

Disappointments are bound to happen, but it is how you handle them that matters. Disappointments and satisfactions are keys on the key chain called life. The keys of satisfaction unlock doors you currently have access, while the keys of disappointments open doors you no longer have access. To prevent your keyring from becoming too heavy and weighing you down, remove the old keys to the doors in your life that are no longer in existence. When you hold on to keys of disappointments, you can find yourself buried under a pile of unnecessary pains, hurts, sorrows, and stress. The trick is to stay in worship to remain in an attitude of prayer - focused on God. The more your eyes are on him, the more dirt that falls off, and the more you attract the blessings of satisfaction.

Today I challenge you to **drop the keys of disappointments**.

When was the last time you were disappointed? How did that event change your perspective on life?

I was disappointed when…	My Perspective Changed because…	Date

A Prayer for Today

Dear Yaweh-Nissi (Lord My Banner),

Life is full of disappointments, but I need you to help me let go of those disappointments. Help me not internalize them; instead, help me run to you, dropping them at the altar. Lord God help me to become more like you. Help me to seek Your face and honor you always. I love you so much! In Jesus' name, I pray, Amen.

Blind Spots

"Love wisdom like a sister; make insight a beloved member of your family." - Proverbs 7:4

Overt busyness leads to a multitude of spiritual blind spots. Blind spots are created when you get too focused on completing tasks without consulting the wisdom of God.

Realize that you are already equipped to do the tasks that need to be done, so instead of being in a hurry to complete the task be in a hurry to seek God's face. The more you seek his face the less blind spots you will encounter.

Today's Challenge

Empty your key ring from keys of disappointments. Allow God to protect you and vindicate you. Stay in your prayer closet and allow God to give you keys of satisfaction.

Blind spots can develop in places where God said **WAIT** and you say **RACE**. Stop trying to rush God into delivering your promise before it has matured into your blessing. When you wait on God, he can give you the wisdom to avoid blind spots and knowledge to embrace the blessing.

Ultimately, spiritual blind spots are indicators that you need to slow down and pay attention to God. As you go through life, do not be so focused on completing tasks that you miss God.

Today, **slow down, take your time, pray, and ask God to help** you be spiritually critical asking for His wisdom at every turn. Take the time to **meditate** on the Word of God and **seek** God for wisdom.

What areas in your life are you spiritually blind?

_____

_____

_____

_____

How would you like God to open your vision?

_____

_____

_____

_____

A Prayer for Today

Dear El-Roi (God Who Sees),

Whatever is blocking my spiritual vision, please remove the hindrance from my field of view. Lord, I want to see what you see - give me eyes to see what you have for me. Give me the heart to follow you and the ability to seek your face in ways I would have never experienced. Lord, help me to focus more on you than the tasks I must complete. Sometimes I am too busy doing what I want to do that I miss you. Lord, teach me to follow you and truly surrender. I cannot be successful without you, so lead me, God, as I surrender to you. In Jesus' name, I pray, Amen.

Drop the Anchor of Unforgiveness

"I will take revenge; I will pay them back. In due time their feet will slip. Their day of disaster will arrive, and their destiny will overtake them." - Deuteronomy 32:35

Like the weight of a ship's anchor, holding grudges and unforgiveness will weigh you down. The weight will prevent you from advancing to the places that God has for you to explore.

Today's Challenge

Choose to let go and forgive. Take an unbothered position and rest in God's Prescence.

When you hold grudges and unforgiveness you are hindering your spiritual growth and maturity. Forgiveness is hard and nobody wants to do it, but it is necessary. It is important to remember that when God asks you to forgive (or let stuff go) it is not for the other person rather it is for yourself. The truth is the quicker you forgive, let go, and allow God to fight your battles the quicker your heart becomes free. True freedom can only be experienced when you are no longer shackled with unforgiveness.

No matter how mad or hurt you are - pray and ask God to create in you a pure heart. God can then work in you and transform you. Regardless of what happens in your life, forgive continuously (Matthew 18:21).

Now understand, forgiveness is not a permission slip to be a doormat, but it is an opportunity for God to fight your battles. The bible says that vengeance is the Lords (Romans 12:19). In other words, God can get your enemies better than you ever could, do not fight people shake the dust off your feet and release that foolishness. The quicker you let go the more time you can focus on what God has for you and what task he has for you to complete. Today I challenge you to **let go and let God**!

Who do you need to forgive today? Write a letter to them expressing how you feel, pray over it - then LET IT GO!

_____

_____

_____

_____

_____

_____

_____

_____

_____

A Prayer for Today

Dear Adonai (Lord),

Help me to forgive those who have come against me. Lord, you said in your word vengeance is yours, not mine. Help me not to react but to respond in love. I know this battle is not mine, but it is yours! I desire to keep maturing spiritually to release all the pain and hurt that I carry! Lord, I surrender! In Jesus' name, I pray, amen.

Weekly Declarations

1. I Declare that I am stepping into spiritual maturity!
2. I Declare that I have a forgiving heart and will not take vengeance in my own hands!
3. I Declare that I will allow God to fight my battles!
4. I Declare that I will rest in the shadow of Gods wings!
5. I Declare that I have 20x20 vision in the spirit allowing me to see the movements of God in my life!
6. I Declare that I run to the altar of Christ Jesus and allow him to alter my situations!
7. I Declare that I go to God first before I go to anyone else!
8. I Declare that I carry Gods light weight; He carries my heavy weight!
9. I Declare that I am emotionally stable!
10. I Declare that I am clothed with the love and favor of Christ Jesus!

Write your own Declarations here...

1.

2.

3.

4.

5.

6.

7.

8.

9.

10.

Week 4

Expecting Manifestations

The Wait

"This vision is for a future time. It describes the end, and it will be fulfilled. If it seems slow in coming, wait patiently, for it will surely take place. It will not be delayed." - Matthew 6:6

When God asks you to wait on him to complete a promise, he is not asking you to sit in the corner like a lost puppy waiting for his owner to come home from work. No, God is asking you to prepare and get ready for the promise.

Today's Challenge

Wait in expectancy for the arrival of the promise.

The key to waiting is seeking his face and preparing for the doors to open. The longer you sit by the door in anticipation, the longer it will take for the promise to arrive. The more you diligently prepare, the more you attract the promise – this is called waiting with expectancy.

6 steps to Waiting in Expectancy:

1. Seek God's face, ask God for wisdom and strategy.
2. Get vulnerable with God, tell him what is on your heart.
3. Ask God to heal your soul wounds.
4. Ask God to help you to let go of the people that have hurt you.
5. Pray for your enemies, your family, and your friends.
6. Keep your eyes on him, not on your problem or the expected promise!
7. Pray, praise, and worship God continuously!
8. Do not listen to naysayers and unsolicited Holy Ghost advice!
9. Prepare! Whatever you are believing for - start preparing for its arrival!
10. Recognize that God is baking a cake for you! Get Ready it is almost done!

Write out a plan on how you will strategically wait for God to manifest the promises.

_____

_____

_____

_____

_____

_____

_____

_____

_____

A Prayer for Today

Dear Jehovah Jireh (God My Provider),

I love you so much. I know you are a promise keeper. I know that when you give me a promise that you will surely bring it to completion. I thank you that supernatural solutions and promises are being delivered to my doorstep today! Lord, I ask that you give me strategies to wait! Teach me to seek your face as I wait! In Jesus' name, I pray, Amen.

Hands Raised and Eyes on God

"I will praise you as long as I live, lifting up my hands to you in prayer."
- Psalm 63:4

One of the best ways to wait for a promise is to adorn God with praise and worship. The more time you spend on your knees with your hands raised and eyes on him, the more you attract his promises (Matthew 6:33).

Today's Challenge

Find three things to be grateful for today. Gratefulness is the key to attracting the promise.

Did you know whining and complaining slows down the arrival speed of your promise? The key to any waiting season is to wait with a purpose! Give God his space to work and ask him to give you H.O.B.B.Y. as you wait. Ask God to give you a Healing, Opportunity, By, Blessing others, and Yielding to God (H.O.B.B.Y.).

During the season of waiting, be sure that you do not wait by yourself. Find members of your *Crazy Faith Holy Ghost Crew* to help keep your hands lifted towards God. In Exodus 17:12, Moses grew weary in fighting the battle, but his *Crazy Faith Holy Ghost Crew* (Aaron and Hur) supported him until the battle was won. Life is not meant to be lived in solitude but community. The people in your community are there to help keep your hands raised and eyes focused on God.

Regardless of the wait time or how possible the situation looks, keep your hands raised in the act of surrender to God, having an attitude of gratitude. Even when you get tired and want to give up, keep your hands raise towards Him and follow the leading of the Holy Spirit.

Today ask God to **give you a H.O.B.B.Y.** as you wait and keep your eyes focused on him and your hands raised.

Gratefulness is one way in which you can keep your hands raised toward heaven and your eyes toward God. Make a list of a few things are grateful for today.

_____

_____

_____

_____

_____

A Prayer for Today

Dear Yahweh-Shalom (Lord My Peace),

Waiting is hard. Honestly, I do not want to wait – I want my promise now. But God, I know you know best and that you will deliver the promise in your timing – not mine. Lord, help me to keep my eyes on you and my hands raised in praise today. Lord, I also ask that you give me a H.O.B.BY while I wait - a Healing, Opportunity, By, Blessing others, and Yielding to you (H.O.B.B.Y.). Lord, as I wait, help me to know you deeper - develop my heart to be more like yours! In Jesus name, I pray, Amen!

Stop Telling God What You're Ready For

"My thoughts are nothing like your thoughts," says the Lord. *"And my ways are far beyond anything you could imagine. For just as the heavens are higher than the earth, so my ways are higher than your ways and my thoughts higher than your thoughts."* - Isaiah 55:8-9

Stop telling God that you are ready for the promise to arrive. God knows the right time and season to deliver the promise. If the promise is slow in coming that means you are not ready for the promise and the promise is not ready for you. Do not grow weary keep praying and praising. Know that God is a promise keeper!

Today's Challenge

Prepare for the promises arrival.

While you are waiting for God to move on your behalf and manifest the promise, start preparing for its arrival. Remember not to be in a hurry that you fail to embrace the process. The lesson learned during the process will prepare you for the promise. Stop being in a big hurry to get to the promise that you fail to pay attention during the process.

The process has keys that will unlock doors for your future. Stop begging, whining, and complaining to God for an early delivery. Your baby is still maturing. God is a good Father, and he will make you wait until you are truly ready. He knows that if he gives you the promise too early, you will ruin what He is trying to get to you and through you.

While you wait, stand against fear. Fear can prevent you from reaching new heights in God's Kingdom. If you let it fear will keep you from the places God is trying to take you. Today I challenge you to **allow God to prepare you** for the next stage of your life. While you wait, stop telling God that you are ready for the promise's arrival and embrace the moment you are in right now.

Instead of telling God when to deliver your promise how about you start preparing for the promise to be delivered. Write down a plan of action that will help you prepare for the promise.

_____

_____

_____

_____

_____

_____

_____

A Prayer for Today

Dear Yahweh-Tsidkenu (Lord Our Righteousness),

Obviously, I do not know what I am ready for, but you do. I know I have tried to tell you what to do in the past, but that has never worked out for me. So today, I want to try something different: lead me into my promise land at your intended time. Open new doors of opportunity according to your timing. I do not want to rush the process; instead, I would like you to learn through the process. Lord, I surrender to you. In Jesus' name, I pray, amen!

Mind Gods Business

"Seek the Kingdom of God [a] above all else, and live righteously, and he will give you everything you need." - Matthew 6:33

God is a jealous God. He does not like it when you divide your attention between him and the world. The more you seek God's face, the more you attract God's hand in your life.

> **Today's Challenge**
>
> Seek Gods face. Ask God what can you do for Him today?

God desires to bless you more than anything, but He wants to be sure that He can trust you before he delivers the promise. He wants to know if you are out for what He can give you or are committed to His business.

The more you seek God's face and "Mind God's business" instead of your own, the more you attract all that he has for you.

The Kingdom of God is not a Burger King with the motto "Have it your way." No, the Kingdom of God is a spiritual land built on the law of attraction. The more you do for God, the more he does for you. The more you focus on him, his will, and bringing more people into the kingdom than the more God is willing to do for and through you.

If God gives you the promise to early before you have reached spiritual maturity, then you will leave Him by the wayside. God does not want to feel used and abused. He wants a relationship with you grounded in intimacy and communion rather than give me, give me, give me. Spiritual maturity is understanding that instead of telling God what he can do for you, you ask God what you can do for him. Today I challenge you to **ask God what I can do for you** rather than God do this for me today.

Describe how you plan to "mind God's business" today?

_____

_____

_____

_____

_____

_____

_____

_____

A Prayer for Today

Dear El-Olam (Everlasting God),

Help me to mind your business more than I mind my own business! To be honest, sometimes I forget that you desire intimacy with me – I get so caught up in my wants that I miss opportunities to commune with you. God teach me to seek you more than I seek the promise. God help me to mature spiritually so that I can become more like you. Help me not to be selfish that I miss opportunities to serve you. Forgive me, God. In Jesus' name, I pray, Amen.

Divine Confirmations

"Then Gideon said to God, "If you are truly going to use me to rescue Israel as you promised, prove it to me in this way...then I will know that you are going to help me rescue Israel as you promised." – Judges 6:36-37

In 2001, Squire Rushnell authored a book entitled God Winks. Throughout the book, Rushnell identifies ways in which God speaks and confirms the very thing God has promised. He describes these soft spiritual encounters as God Winks.

Today's Challenge

Be in expectancy for a confirmation of the promise's arrival.

From experience, these encounters are often as subtle as a little sparrow or as blatant as a billboard on top of a large building. Every spiritual encounter has a connection to God's providence. Though you cannot physically see what God is doing, do not lose faith! Keep praying and keep being in expectancy for the arrival of the promise.

The story of Gideon is a prime example of God's divine confirmation. Gideon asks God to provide several assurances to ensure that he would not go alone into a losing battle. God uses confirmation after confirmation to confirm the promise.

Divine confirmations are God's way of confirming that He did not forget about you and that He is working on your behalf! As a child of God, He knows you very well; every now and then, he sends you a reminder of his love and evidence that the promise is closer than you think!

While you wait, keep your spiritual eyes open for divine confirmations to let you know that the promise is on the way. Today I challenge you to **ask God to confirm the promises' arrival** and when you get the confirmation, give thanks!

Be bold like Gideon and ask God to give you a divine confirmation of God's promise to you.

Gods Promise to You	Divine Confirmation	Date

A Prayer for Today

Dear El-Roi (God Who Sees),

Remove the spiritual veil off my eyes so that I may experience your divine confirmations. Give me divine clarity and wisdom to pursue my God-given assignment for my life. In Jesus' name, I pray, Amen.

Do Not Be So Easily Offended

"Sensible people control their temper; they earn respect by overlooking wrongs." - Proverbs 19:11

As a child of God, you cannot allow the emotional instability of others to move you from a place of emotional stability with God. It Is important to remember that people's reactions have absolutely nothing to do with you and everything to do with what the other person is dealing with outside of your interactions.

> **Today's Challenge**
>
> Seek to keep your peace even when storms are brewing from others.

As a child of the King, remember not to be so easily offended. Develop thick Holy Ghost alligator skin to protect you against the nonsense of the world. As you proceed thru life and life challenges let all the drama roll off your back like water on a duck's back.

Allow God to protect your heart. Instead of spending time sulking in hurt feelings run to the cross – place yourself at the throne room of heaven. Begin to praise God, worship him, and ask him for wisdom on how to proceed. God hears your every prayer, and he sees your heart.

Another thing to remember is that if you died tomorrow from the stress of carrying offense against someone, that same someone will move on without remorse. In all honesty for your health and sanity you are better off shaking the dust off your feet and moving on to complete your God given assignments.

Today I challenge you to **control** your temper, **regulate** your heart, and **overlook** the wrongs of others. Give the hurt to God and go live your best life!

When was the last time you were offended and why? Was it worth the time and effort you spent concerned about it?

Offense	Why?	Worth your Concern? (Y/N)

A Prayer for Today

Dear Yahweh- Shalom (God of Peace),

Help me to not be so easily offended. Give me blinders against the offense. Help me to see people and situations from your point of view not my own. In Jesus' name, I pray, Amen.

Full Circle Moments

"And I am certain that God, who began the good work within you, will continue his work until it is finally finished on the day when Christ Jesus returns." Philippians 1:6

A full-circle moment is a point in time where God brings everything back to the position in which you left off. In one sense a full circle moment is God's grace allowing you to repeat what you did not get right the first time.

Today's Challenge

Ask God to give you full circle moments, specifically in areas where it seems the promise is dead.

Jesus is probably one of the most significant examples of a full-circle moment in the Bible. The origin of the circle begins in the Old Testament, where the stories point directly to the birth and resurrection of Jesus in the New Testament. The New Testament is where the circle is completed - the first promise God gave manifested. Essentially everything in the Bible comes to a full circle.

Full circle moments are God's unique way of giving you a second chance to access the promises you evaded. When you make a mistake and find yourself running like Jonah from God's purpose, He has a way of bringing everything full circle. The truth is that when God makes a promise, no one can take that promise from you, not even you. Every promise God makes is a covenant, this means it cannot be broken. God is a promise keeper. If something is for you, then nothing can stop you from reaching that promise. No matter how long it takes, God has a way of bringing everything back to a full circle.

Today I challenge you to **expect and embrace full circle moments**. Do not let anything stop you from getting to the places God has for you to obtain. You are special to God!

What are you expecting God to bring full circle in your life?

_____

_____

_____

_____

_____

_____

_____

_____

A Prayer for Today

Dear El Deah (God of Knowledge),

Give me wisdom and discernment to respond rather than react when I face challenges. Teach me to follow your voice rather than following my own. God, I know you are in control – help me fully mature to access the places you have called me to be. Lord, I love you, and I surrender to you as you bring everything full circle. In Jesus name, I pray, amen.

Weekly Declarations

1. I Declare that my manifestations are arriving right on time!
2. I Declare that I am waiting with an attitude of preparation!
3. I Declare that I am maturing in Christ Jesus!
4. I Declare that I am not easily offended!
5. I Declare that all spiritual veils are removed from my eyes!
6. I Declare that I mind God's business and allow God to mind my business! I surrender to Christ Jesus!
7. I Declare that I am in right standing with Christ Jesus!
8. I Declare that God is giving me full circle moments!
9. I Declare that I am entering into a season of accelerated completion!
10. I Declare that the wait is over, and my manifestations are here!

Write your own Declarations here...

1.

2.

3.

4.

5.

6.

7.

8.

9.

10.

Sinners Prayer

"For this is how God loved the world: He gave[a] his one and only Son, so that everyone who believes in him will not perish but have eternal life. - John 3:16

Dear El Elyon (God Most High),

Today I surrender my life to you. I know that I miss the target sometimes and do not get everything right. I realize that I cannot do anything without you, and I am tired of trying. Today, I ask that you come into my life and save me. Teach me to be more like you and walk in your way.

Today I accept your son Jesus to live on the inside of me. I ask that you teach me to walk like Christ in all that I do. Transform my heart and my soul as I commit my life to you. In Jesus' name, I pray, Amen!

About the Author

Joy Semien is an award-winning author and presenter. She holds a Bachelor of Science degree from Dillard University (2015) in Biology with a minor in Chemistry. Joy holds a master's degree from Texas Southern University (2017) in Urban Planning and Environmental Policy. She also holds a ministerial diploma from *Ever Increasing Word Training Center (2017)* under the leadership of Apostle Leroy Thompson.

In 2020, Joy founded *The Holy Ghost and Me* ministry crossover. The crossover is a subsidiary of L.E.E.D. With Joy LLC, whose mission is centered around Listening, Engaging, Empowering, and Driving Change. Through the crossover, Joy seeks to teach people how to establish a solid relationship with the one who made them (GOD) through periodic blogging, vlogging, and podcasting.

To learn more about Joy and L.E.E.D. With Joy visit https://leedingwithjoy.com. To learn more about The Holy Ghost and Me visit the website https://theholyghostandme.net, follow @theholyghostandme on Instagram, Facebook, and YouTube.

www.ingramcontent.com/pod-product-compliance
Lightning Source LLC
Chambersburg PA
CBHW042332150426
43194CB00001B/28

Establish Your Holy Ghost Crew

"But the Lord told Gideon, "There are still too many! Bring them down to the spring, and I will test them to determine who will go with you and who will not." – Judges 7:4

Every army commander has a crew of men/women whom they will lead into battle. The crew is often tasked with listening and executing the commander's battle plans. As they go into enemy territory, the crew is tasked with covering each other and the commander.

Today's Challenge

Identify members of your Holy Ghost Crew.

In your personal life, you should have a similar crew, the "*Crazy Faith Holy Ghost Crew*"! This crew is not just your primary set of friends, the ones you call BFF's or your closest family members. The truth is that many of your closest friends/family members cannot hang with you in spiritual fights - they will hold you back, just ask Gideon. The quicker you realize that some people in your life are unequipped to walk through the fires with you, the faster you can identify those who are designed to be a part of your *Crazy Faith Holy Ghost Crew*.

Members of your *Crazy Faith Holy Ghost Crew* should be people who always have your back in the spirit - even when the battleplan looks unsuccessful. Members of this crew are typically non-traditional, they never ask burden-based questions, never offer their doubt nor provide unsolicited Holy Ghost advice. Instead, they pray, worship, encourage, and spiritually push you into your destiny. They will cover you while in enemy territory, notifying you of blind spots and landmines. Today take the time to **identify** members of your Holy Ghost Crew. **Ask God** to **remove** those **people** in your life who do not need to be there.

Make a list of people in your life. Place a plus sign by those who are adding value and a subtraction sign by those who are subtracting value.

Note: Those who are adding value should be members of your *Crazy Faith Holy Ghost Crew*, everyone else should just play the background.

Name of Person	Add Value (+)	Subtract Value (-)

A Prayer for Today

Dear El-Roi (God Who Sees),

Today I ask that you help me identify the people in my life who is or should be part of my Holy Ghost Crew! God, I ask that you remove, replace, and replenish the people in my life who do not need to be a part of my next level. Remove those who hinder me from operating in my purpose. For those who remain, help us to encourage each other and grow together spiritually. Lord, I welcome your wisdom and discernment. In Jesus' name, I pray, Amen!

Prayers of a Warrior

"Then if my people who are called by my name will humble themselves and pray and seek my face and turn from their wicked ways, I will hear from heaven and will forgive their sins and restore their land." – 2 Chronicles 7:14

True Warriors or experienced soldiers. They have been to battle and have developed the skills needed to defeat their enemies – but most importantly they know how to listen to the voice of the commander.

> **Today's Challenge**
>
> Mimic the walk of Jehoshaphat, praying and fasting until God answers your prayers.

Jehoshaphat is a prime example from the Bible of a warrior who knew how to activate his authority through prayer. Before he would go into battle, he would pray for direction. Ultimately, Jehoshaphat took his worries and anxieties to the throne and did not leave God's presence until he had his answer. After receiving the order from God, he played no games enforcing God's will.

Jehoshaphat's willingness and obedience led to many wins throughout his reign. He knew he would see an immediate response after fasting and praying. Mathew 17:21 says that some demonic attacks are only removed through fasting and praying. Fasting scrambles, the plans of the enemy and releases heaven on earth.

As you prepare for battle realize you enter the battle from a place of victory! You are the child of a King, designed to WIN! You have all authority to defeat the devil and his little minions! There is not a demon in hell that can take you out unless you let him. So today **DO NOT** let that nasty devil have even a foothold in your life!

Write down the areas in your life that you need God to move (prayer target). Begin to pray over these areas daily and expect God to move on your behalf.

Prayer Target	Scripture for Battle

A Prayer for Today

Dear Yahweh-Tsabbaoth (Lord of Host),

Thank you for who you are and all that you are! Lord thank you for your greatness! God, I know that this battle is yours and not mine! I know that you are working on my behalf! Lord, today I surrender all my worries and anxieties to you. Take the wheel God because I know without you all my plans will fail. In Jesus name, I pray, Amen.